Seymour Simon

BIG BUGS

SCHOLASTIC INC.

New York Toronto London Auckland Sydney
Mexico City New Delhi Hong Kong Buenos Aires

To Benjamin and Joel

Front cover photograph: praying mantis

Title page photograph: lantern fly

Page 3 photograph: dragonfly

Permission to use the following photographs is gratefully acknowledged:

Front cover: © Tim Davis/Photo Researchers, Inc.; title page, pages 14–15: © Gary Retherford/Photo Researchers, Inc.; pages 2–3, 18–19: © Stephen Dalton/Photo Researchers, Inc.; pages 4–5, 16–17: © John Mitchell/Photo Researchers, Inc.; pages 6–7: © Bob Jensen/Bruce Coleman Inc.; pages 8–9, 20–21: © Gail Shumway/Bruce Coleman Inc.; pages 10–11: © Jane Burton/Bruce Coleman Inc.; pages 12–13: © Robert Shantz; pages 22–23: © Jeff Lepore/Photo Researchers, Inc.; pages 24–25:©Michael Lustbader/Photo Researchers, Inc.; pages 26–27: © Michael Fogden/AnimalsAnimals; pages 28–29: © John Mitchell/OSF/AnimalsAnimals; pages 30–31: © Tom McHugh/Photo Researchers, Inc.; page 32: © Michael Fogden/Bruce Coleman Inc; back cover: © David M. Dennis/AnimalsAnimals

ISBN 0-439-85183-1

12 11 10 9 8 7 6 5 4 3 2 1   6 7 8 9 10 11/0

Printed in the U.S.A.   23

First Scholastic printing, February 2006

Book design by E. Friedman.
Typeset in 22/40 ITC Century Book.

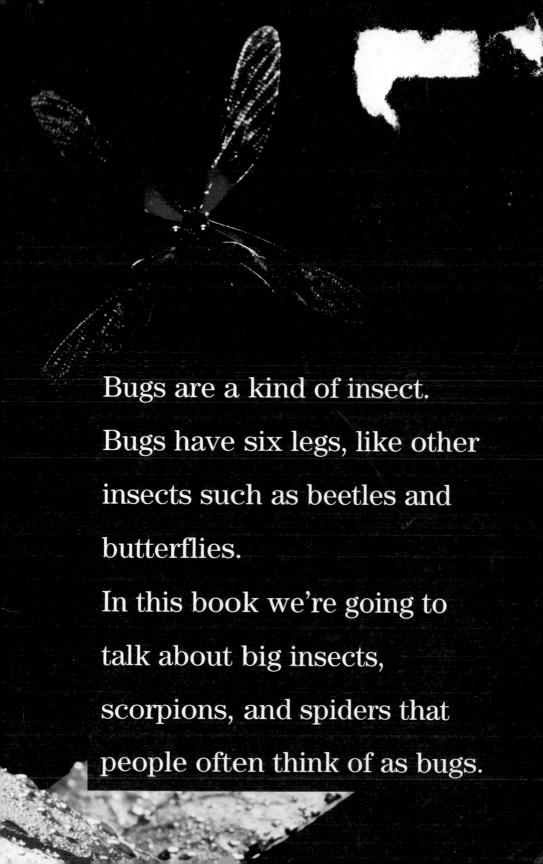

Bugs are a kind of insect. Bugs have six legs, like other insects such as beetles and butterflies. In this book we're going to talk about big insects, scorpions, and spiders that people often think of as bugs.

The giant water
bug is the largest
bug in the world.
A giant water bug
can kill a frog or
a fish twice its size.

The goliath beetle of West Africa is the heaviest insect in the world. It is over 4 inches long and weighs nearly $\frac{1}{4}$ pound. That's about the size of an apple.

Despite their weight, goliath beetles
are able to fly.

They zip through the air like
bullets and can break glass windows.

Actual size

The giant cockroach of South America is the largest roach in the world.

Actual size

It is about 3 inches long.

It gives off an awful smell so it won't be eaten by its enemies.

But some people keep giant cockroaches as pets.

The bulldog ant of Australia is about 1½ inches long, about the size of your pinky. This ant has powerful jaws and a mean sting. Bulldog ants will attack anything that comes near their nest.

Actual Size

The female tarantula-hawk wasp stings a tarantula and paralyzes it. She lays her eggs on the tarantula.

Actual size

The eggs hatch in several days, and the young wasps feed on the body of the tarantula.

The lantern fly of South America

is about 3 inches long.

The top of its head looks

like an alligator.

The top of its head is

also hollow, like a peanut shell.

No one knows why.

Actual size

Robber flies can grow
to be 2 inches long,
with a 4-inch wingspan.
They hunt any flying
insect, even bees
and wasps.
The largest robber flies live
in South America or
Australia, but many large
robber flies live in the
United States.

Actual size

Huge dragonflies lived over 300 million years ago, long before the dinosaurs.

They had wingspans of 30 inches, about the length of a person's arm.

Most dragonflies today have wingspans of 3 or 4 inches.

Dragonflies are great fliers and can catch and eat insects in midair.

Birdwing butterflies are the biggest butterflies in the world. These colorful giants from Australia have a 12-inch wingspan.

They fly so fast that people can't catch them with nets. Instead, collectors try to knock them down with a blast of water.

Atlas is the name of a giant in early Greek legends. The atlas moth of Southeast Asia has a larger wing area than any other moth. Its wings cover about the same space as two pages of this book.

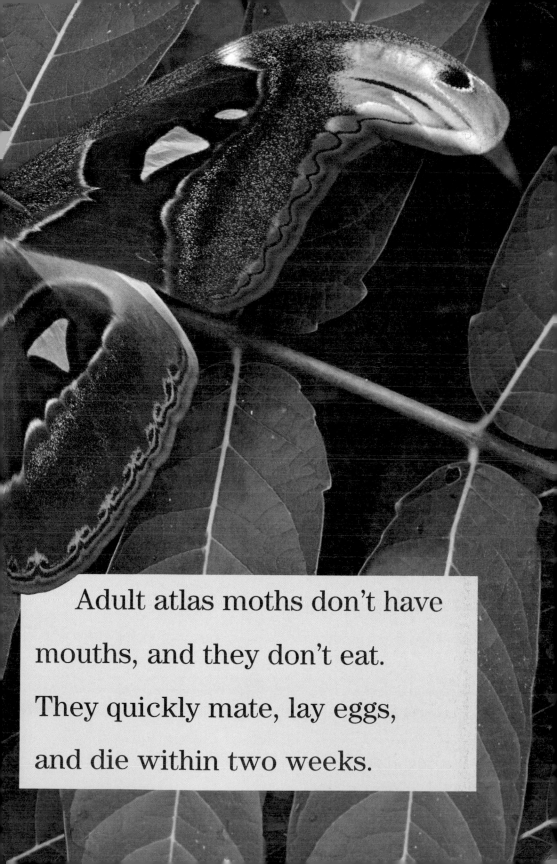

Adult atlas moths don't have mouths, and they don't eat. They quickly mate, lay eggs, and die within two weeks.

A praying mantis doesn't pray.
It is really waiting quietly for an
insect to pass by.
When a mantis catches an insect,
it feeds on it like a person eating
an ear of corn.

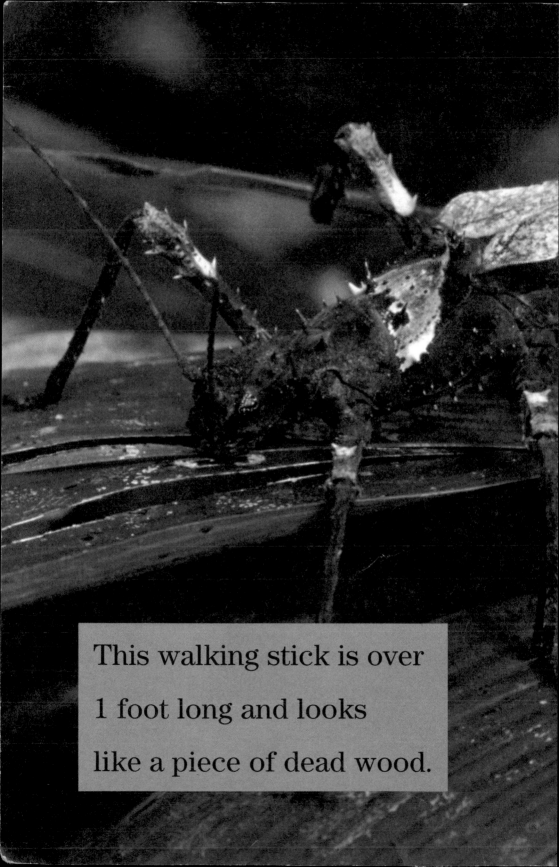

This walking stick is over 1 foot long and looks like a piece of dead wood.

It moves slowly at night and feeds on leaves.

Lizards, birds, and spiders will eat walking sticks, but they have a hard time spotting them.

The bird-eating spider of South America is the biggest spider in the world.

It is as large as your open hand. Bird-eating spiders catch and eat birds and other small animals.

An African giant
scorpion can grow
to be 8 inches long.

The giant scorpion hunts for insects at night and tears them to pieces with its large claws.

Most bugs are tiny and weigh about as much as a feather.

The bugs in this book weigh dozens of times more than most other bugs.

That is why we call them big bugs.